Emily's Shoes

Written and Illustrated
by Joan Cottle

Children's Press®
A Division of Grolier Publishing
New York • London • Hong Kong • Sydney
Danbury, Connecticut

For my cousin, Teresa

Reading Consultants
Linda Cornwell
Coordinator of School Quality and Professional Improvement
(Indiana State Teachers Association)

Katharine A. Kane
Education Consultant
(Retired, San Diego County Office of Education
and San Diego State University)

Visit Children's Press® on the Internet at:
http://publishing.grolier.com

Library of Congress Cataloging-in-Publication Data
Cottle, Joan.
  Emily's shoes / written by Joan Cottle; illustrated by Joan Cottle.
    p. cm. — (Rookie reader)
  Summary: When her mother calls her, a young girl tries to guess what type of
shoes she needs to wear.
  ISBN 0-516-21585-X (lib.bdg.)   0-516-26544-X (pbk.)
  1. Shoes—Fiction. I. Cottle, Joan, ill. II. Title. III. Series.
PZ7.C8294Em 1999
[E]—dc21
                                                            98-53054
                                                            CIP
                                                            AC

GROLIER
PUBLISHING 1 2 3 4 5 6 7 8 9 10 R 08 07 06 05 04 03 02 01 00 99

"Emily, it's time!" said Mom.

3

"For what?" Emily wondered.
"For the party?"

"For soccer?"

11

"For ballet?"

13

"For a sleep-over?"

19

"For ice-skating?"

21

"For a hike?"

26

"You don't need any shoes,"
said Mom.

"Why?" Emily asked.
"What time is it?"

"It's bathtime!"

31

WORD LIST (27 words)

a	hike	shoes
any	ice-skating	sleep-over
asked	is	soccer
ballet	it	the
bathtime	it's	time
don't	Mom	what
Emily	need	why
Emily's	party	wondered
for	said	you

ABOUT THE AUTHOR

Joan Cottle grew up in Connecticut and studied painting at Boston University where she received her Master's Degree in Fine Art. She lives in Los Gatos, California, with her husband, two children, and her yellow Labrador, who is her loyal studio companion. Joan has illustrated several books including How Many Ants? by Larry Dane Brimner in the Rookie Reader series. Emily's Shoes is Joan first book as both author and illustrator.